THE PULLMAN STRIKE OF 1894

American Labor Comes of Age

Great Events

THE PULLMAN
STRIKE OF 1894

American Labor Comes of Age

Rosemary Laughlin

**MORGAN
REYNOLDS
Incorporated**

Greensboro

THE PULLMAN STRIKE OF 1894
American Labor Comes of Age

Photos courtesy
Illinois State Historical Library,
Chicago Public Library,
Newberry Library - Chicago, Illinois,
Eugene V. Debs Foundation - Terre Haute, Indiana

Cover Photo courtesy
Illinois State Historical Library.

Library of Congress Cataloging-in-Publication Data
Laughlin, Rosemary
     The Pullman strike of 1894 : American labor comes of age /
Rosemary Laughlin.
         p. cm. -- (Great events)
     Includes bibliographical references and index.
     ISBN 1-883846-28-5
     1. Chicago Strike, 1894. 2. Strikes and lockouts--Railroads.
3. Railroads--History. 4. Labor movement--Illinois--Chicago.
I. Title. II. Series.
HD5325.R12 1894.C5395   1999
331.892'8523'0977311--dc21   99-25695
                                                              CIP

To
Pat and Tony

Contents

Chapter One

    Strike! 9

Chapter Two

    Labor and the Railroads 13

Chapter Three

    Owners and Managers: The Other Side 21

Chapter Four

    How the Strike Spread 34

Chapter Five

    The Strike Moves Beyond Pullman .55

Chapter Six

    Debs and the Law 64

Chapter Seven

    The United States Strike Commission 73

Chapter Eight

    The Pullman Strike's Role in U.S. History 85

Glossary 98

Timeline 102

Bibliography 108

Index 110

A Pullman Lounge Car

Chapter One

Strike!

Worries and fears crackled like static electricity among the workers inside the Pullman Palace Car Company on the morning of May 11, 1894:

"We're going to be locked out! Pullman doesn't want the word to spread that there's to be a vote whether to strike or not!"

"What do we do now? Pick up another paycheck for seven cents and live on air?"

"If only Pullman would reduce cottage rents, we might make it!"

"If the company would stop letting our forewoman grind us down with abuse and cheaper piece-work rates! She doesn't care if a girl is sick or doesn't make enough to live! She just figures to make the department look good to the superintendent."

Painters, seamstresses, car builders, steam-fitters, electrical technicians, mechanics, wood trimmers, and assorted helpers all felt upset and anxious. They were desperate and ready to do something.

The union representatives told the workers to stop work, go outside, and vote on whether they wanted to strike. Like a giant wave, three thousand workers laid down their tools and left the building. Three hundred remained, mostly clerks and foremen.

In a nearby meeting hall the workers voted to strike. They did so because they felt there was no other way to convince George Pullman of their plight. For a year their pay rates had steadily declined, and their work hours were reduced while the price of food and rent did not decrease. Their families were hungry and sick. They were simply not earning enough to live on.

Union rules required a vote of all members for a strike, the dreaded word that meant they would stop work—and receive no pay—until an agreement that allowed them to come back to work under better conditions was made with Mr. Pullman, their employer.

The workers had talked to Mr. Pullman earlier. He told them business was bad and that he was keeping the factory open just to give them what work he could scrape up. However, the pay of all Pullman officials, superintendents, and foremen had not been reduced. Stock dividends were still being paid to shareholders. When asked if he would allow a board of neutral judges to decide what should be done that was fair to everyone, Pullman refused. Repeatedly he insisted, "There is nothing to arbitrate."

On May 10, 1894, three of the employees who had

met with Mr. Pullman were laid off. The workers feared that these three—there had been forty-six in all—were being punished because of the requests they had made and for criticizing certain superintendents. They thought Mr. Pullman saw them as rebellious and threatening, of being the ringleaders of a strike movement. Later it would be clarified that the lay-offs of these three were an unfortunate coincidence, but in the tension of the moment, the workers concluded they had been fired for speaking out. The rumor spread that the three had permanently lost their jobs.

The night of May 10 union representatives met to decide what to do before more workers lost their jobs. This meeting lasted until five o'clock the next morning. They agreed unity of action was essential and organized an election to vote on whether they should strike or not.

The strikers then created a central committee that would meet daily in a public hall and act as a clearinghouse for all problems. Food and medical services were already needed, and now these would have to come from the charity of others. The response from church groups and sympathizers in Chicago was supportive and generous.

The committee's other major concern was violence. The strikers were committed to a peaceful solution and abhorred the possibility of vandalism or destruction at the Pullman plant by angry individuals or hoodlums from Chicago. Any violence would only hurt their cause by allowing Pullman to condemn them for being an unruly mob. They organized three hundred strikers to set up twenty-four hour watches at various locations around the locked-up buildings.

This was the beginning of the Pullman Strike of 1894, also called the Chicago Strike. It lasted for two months and was full of unexpected and dramatic developments. Soon the direct effects of the strike would spread to twenty-seven states and territories. It was to become a landmark in the history of relations between workers and factory owners in the United States.

The Pullman Strike was a major battle between working people and corporation owners. President Grover Cleveland called it "unusual and especially per-plexing," giving him the "most troublous and anxious" time of his administration. The strike proved that large numbers of sympathetic workers would actively sup-port other workers who went out on strike. It also reflected the ongoing dispute between states' rights and federal powers. It defined new ways for state and fed-eral governments to intervene in transportation and commerce.

How did this watershed disruption of the American economy come about? The best way to begin to under-stand the 1894 strike is to look at how the relationship between workers and management had developed in the decades after the Civil War.

Chapter Two

Labor and the Railroads

Before the Civil War, which lasted from 1861 to 1865, the standard working day in an American factory was at least ten hours for skilled workers, and twelve to fourteen hours for unskilled laborers, including women and children. After the Civil War, the number of immigrants in the United States swelled. This influx crowded the big cities like New York and Chicago and provided cheap labor. It also created terrible living conditions in the crowded slums.

These new urban workers slowly began insisting on higher wages. The best, perhaps the only, way to successfully agitate for better treatment from employers was by starting unions. Unions are organized groups of workers, usually determined by the industry they work in (steelworkers, coal miners, etc.,) that negotiate with management or if necessary call upon the workers to go out on strike. Over the years before and after the Civil War there had been attempts to start unions, but these efforts had been squashed by the state and federal courts that labeled them as "conspiracy." In 1842 the Supreme Court held that unions were legal organizations. By 1873 there were thirty national unions, one of which was the Knights of Labor.

The first major railroad strike began on the Baltimore & Ohio Railroad in 1877 after wages were repeatedly cut. Workers were tired of the mergers and monopolies that benefited only a few "robber barons" (owners) while slashing jobs and wages for the workers. The Baltimore & Ohio trains came to a halt, and angry mobs drove out the state troops sent in to restore order. When the governors of Maryland, Illinois, Pennsylvania, and West Virginia asked for federal troops to end the strike, they got them. The strike was crushed in two weeks.

Another strike, the so-called Haymarket Square riots of 1886, involved workers demanding an eight-hour work day at the McCormick reaper factory in Chicago. After three workers were killed by the police, anarchists and bystanders became involved. Their involvement resulted in a bomb and more deaths. This violence outraged the country and the union was blamed for the violence.

In 1892 employees were locked out of the Carnegie Steel Corporation in Homestead, Pennsylvania. The company wanted to deny work to the unionized employees in an attempt to break their union. Three hundred Pinkerton detectives were hired to keep the workers out. When a gun battle began the governor called out the militia. The result was a victory for Carnegie Steel. Only non-union men were hired to work at Carnegie Steel after the Homestead Strike.

During these years of agitation leaders emerged in the union movement. Probably the most important was the cigar maker Samuel Gompers, who became president of his local union and then went on to found the American Federation of Labor (AFL) in 1881. The AFL superceded the Knights of Labor in 1886. Gompers avoided political entanglements, particularly the increasingly popular socialist movement. Instead he stressed "bread and butter" issues that were close to the hearts of the AFL membership: higher wages, shorter hours, and more freedom to advance on the job.

While Gompers shunned socialism, another influential man in labor unions was the leader of America's socialist movement. Eugene Victor Debs believed that socialism, not capitalism, was the preferable way to organize a society. Debs felt that government ownership was more just than private ownership of the means of production (such as factories) and the distribution of goods (such as railroads.) He thought that socialism fostered cooperation and social goodwill while capitalism bred competition and profit at all cost.

Eugene Debs was an idealist, a kind person and an untiring worker for the ideas he believed. One of ten children born in Terre Haute, Indiana to French immi-

Eugene Debs was a powerful union organizer and key figure in the Pullman Strike.

grant parents, he began working in the railroad shops at the age of fifteen and later became a locomotive fireman. He joined the firemen's union, became a union officer, and was the editor for *Firemen's Magazine*. He was eventually elected to be a city clerk in Terre Haute and became a member of the Indiana legislature.

Debs helped found the American Railway Union and was elected president on June 20, 1893. Its goal was to unite the many different single "craft" or "skill" unions together to create one large union for all railroad workers. One year after Debs became president, the American Railway Union had 150,000 members.

Debs and the American Railway Union gained national attention and recognition in April 1894 when James J. Hill of the Great Northern Railroad refused to increase the wages of his employees although they were the lowest paid on the transcontinental lines. The men of the Great Northern Railroad struck, and no trains moved on the Great Northern roads except those carrying mail. (Because mail was a federal function it was illegal for strikers to interfere with its delivery. Management often claimed that striking workers were disrupting the mail in their efforts to force federal intervention against the work stoppage.)

Debs, a powerful, persuasive speaker, addressed the strikers and urged discipline, cooperation and non-violence. His physical appearance—he was over six feet tall and clean-shaven with strong features—enhanced his outgoing personality. His sincere speech was a success with the strikers.

After Debs' speech, Hill agreed to a settlement arranged by the arbitration of fourteen businessmen of Minneapolis and St. Paul. They agreed that wages should be increased, and they were—by a total of $146,000 a month for the Great Northern payroll. The strike was over in eighteen days. The union had won.

Debs was ecstatic over the agreement. To him this was proof that workers and managers could cooperate and that arbitration was the key to a successful strike resolution. When the Pullman Strike occurred a month after the Great Northern strike, he had hopes for the same outcome.

Another figure who would play a role in the upcoming Pullman Strike was Illinois Governor John Peter Altgeld. Although he was never a member of a union, Altgeld was sympathetic to workers. The son of poor German immigrants, he served as a Union soldier in the Civil War. After the war, he moved west, working as a common laborer. He eventually became a teacher. Later he studied law and was elected a state attorney for a Missouri county in 1874.

Altgeld moved to Chicago to practice law and wrote a small book on crime called *Our Penal Machinery and Its Victims* in 1884. In his book he said that the poor had less than a fair chance in American life because crowded cities and low wages bred crime.

Illinois Governor John Peter Altgeld thought that the courts and the government should be more on the side of workers and the poor.

Altgeld thought the courts were not concerned about the welfare of the young men who were filling the jails.

Altgeld was elected to the superior court of Cook County, for which he became the "chief justice." Altgeld became so influential among Illinois Democrats they nominated him for Governor of Illinois in 1892.

Altgeld won the election. After only a few weeks in office he considered three appeals for clemency for convictions dealing with the Haymarket Square riots in 1886. He studied the facts carefully and decided that the judge had been prejudiced and the jury had been "packed" with management sympathizers. Altgeld pardoned the three anarchists convicted for conspiring with the murderers during the riots. He described the evidence and his reasons for the pardon when he issued it, but many people disagreed. He was criticized and attacked in the newspapers.

Altgeld determined at that moment that he would do what he thought was right even if it was not popular. He remained true to this decision when the Pullman Strike broke out a year later.

Chapter Three

Owners and Managers: The Other Side

Eugene Debs represented one side of the debate between workers and management that erupted in the Pullman Strike. He spoke for the workers who wanted a larger portion of the immense wealth they were helping to create in the post-Civil War industrial boom.

George Mortimer Pullman embodied the opposing side of the conflict. In many ways Pullman was an example of what had come to be called the American Dream—the idea that anyone who is hard-working, inventive, and far-sighted can make a great success by participating in the dynamic American economy.

Pullman was one of ten children born to a skilled and hardworking but poor mechanic. He had to quit school at fourteen to work in a store, but continued to study by himself at night. A brother helped him learn cabinetmaking. When the state of New York widened the Erie Canal, Pullman got a job and learned about moving buildings and improving drainage.

When young Pullman learned in 1855 that Chicago needed men to raise streets and buildings on land being eroded by Lake Michigan, he traveled to that growing city. During the long train trip he could not sleep in the cramped, dirty bunk with its lumpy mattress, stuffy air, and constant jolting. He stopped trying to sleep, got up, sat at the end of the car, and thought about possibilities for better sleeping accommodations on trains.

Excited about his idea, Pullman got a position with the Woodruff Sleeping Car Company and helped to convert two regular coaches into sleeping cars. With his cabinetry skills, he supervised the carpenters and worked with them to get exactly what he wanted.

Pullman expected great success from his sleeping car, but it did not come. Temporarily discouraged, he went off to Colorado during the gold rush. He returned to Chicago in 1864 and decided to make his sleeping car idea work again. This time he had a different plan. He spent $20,000 instead of the usual $5,000 for a railroad sleeping car and constructed the Pioneer. The Pioneer was a day-coach that turned into a sleeper at night, with upper berths on shelves that swung into the ceiling. Pullman was careful to make the car very beautiful as well as comfortable.

The Pioneer was one foot wider and two and one-half feet higher than regular cars, so some railroads were not willing to try it at first. Then in 1865 the Pioneer was used by the Chicago & Alton to transport

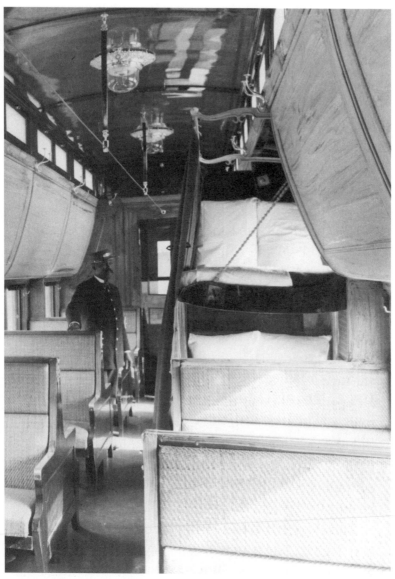

This photo shows how the porter could pull down a berth. All the bedding could be stored in it when it was upright. A Pullman porter stands in the car. Pullman porters were famous for their excellent service and gracious manners.

the body of the assassinated President Lincoln west to Springfield, Illinois. This helped to popularize the new style railroad passenger car.

In 1867 Pullman incorporated the Pullman Palace Car Company in Illinois. It began manufacturing dining cars, parlor cars, and private cars as well as sleepers. Pullman began to sell cars in England, Scotland, and Italy. By 1879 the manufacturing plant in Detroit and the repair units in three other cities were no longer sufficient to handle the increased business. Pullman needed more room to build a larger facility. He decided to build a new factory with a model town around it near Chicago, Illinois.

Pullman wanted to make life healthier and happier for his workers. He thought he could do so and make more money at the same time. He had read about three experimental industrial towns in Europe that had success combining work and home: Saltaire, England; Guise, France; and Essen, Germany. Pullman may have visited Saltaire, where alpaca woolens were manufactured, when he was in England selling his cars. His town greatly resembled Saltaire.

George Pullman chose four thousand acres on the prairie twelve miles south of downtown Chicago. He sought the advice of architects, engineers, and industrial experts while building his town. But most of his advisors did not stay employed with Pullman for long. Although he had a remarkable memory and grasp of

A luxury Pullman car from the late 1890s. Note the highly polished wood, the plush upholstered seats that slid down into a bed, the fringed window shades and elaborate ceiling decorations. Pullman employees were highly skilled in a number of crafts.

detail, his personality was brusque—he was not easy to get along with.

Construction of the town of Pullman, named in honor of the founder himself, began in 1880. The factory shops were built first and by April 1881 were rolling out railroad cars.

Pullman did not cut corners in building the town. He wanted only the best and most advanced features. Cream-colored clay for the bricks was taken from nearby Lake Calumet. An advanced sewer system allowed the sewage to flow by gravity to a reservoir where it was pumped to a basin to be filtered through tiles. The clean water was drained into Lake Calumet and the organic matter was used on a model farm that yielded an eight percent profit from vegetables sold in the town and Chicago. A dairy farm of one hundred cows was also included. There was a gas plant, and ice-houses adjoined it on the shores of Lake Calumet. Heat created in the shops' boilers was piped to warm the public buildings and the better quality residences.

Pullman featured a central square with public buildings and an arcade for the Pullman headquarters and other businesses. The Florence Hotel in Queen Anne style was built with brick, trimmed in stone and roofed with slate. There were also a theater, school, church and library. The library was seldom used because people had to pay a three dollar fee annually. Unlike Andrew Carnegie who built 2800 free libraries,

The Pullman school was surrounded by a playground. It could serve one thousand students.

Pullman believed that people would only appreciate the books if they had to pay to read them.

The church was not used until 1886 because the rent was too high. No other churches were allowed to be built, although fifteen religious denominations rented rooms or were in towns nearby. The town school maintained high standards, and the children of Pullman were guaranteed schooling from kindergarten through eighth grade. An evening school was added to provide high school courses, including mechanical drawing, bookkeeping, and secretarial skills.

George Pullman was perplexed and hurt when his town was criticized as feudal or paternalistic. This means that, as in the Middle Ages, one man owns the land and controls much in the lives of the people who live on it, collecting rent and fees that he alone sets. Pullman felt that since people chose to live in his town, he could not be accused of controlling their lives.

Many of the workers saw it differently. They felt that if they did not live in Pullman, they would not keep their jobs. This made them bitter because rents were higher than for comparable housing in nearby towns. Pullman countered the arguments by pointing out that the town provided many services like mowing the grass and repairing the buildings. He had trouble grasping the fact that others wanted to participate in the economy, just as he did, by owning and maintaining their own homes. This was a strange lack of under-

The Pullman Palace Car Company's Administration building. Note the clock tower to the left. To the right can be seen the four carshops where the majority of employees worked.

standing on the part of Pullman, a strong believer in free enterprise and private property. After a visit to Pullman in 1885, a reporter for the *New York Sun* concluded:

> They [the workers] want to run the municipal government themselves, according to the ordinary American fashion. They secretly rebel because the Pullman Company continues its watch and authority over them after working hours. They declare they are bound hand and foot by a philanthropic monopoly.

George Pullman's paternalism was very unusual and eventually counter-productive. Those who ran the railroads were not interested in their employees' lives apart from work, but they made efforts to control the wages that determined the workers' quality of life.

Another group who participated in the strike were the railroad owners. They created an organization called The General Managers' Association in 1886 for "the consideration of problems of management arising from the operation of railroads terminating or centering in Chicago." There were twenty-four of these lines at that time, including such giant systems as the Illinois Central, the Baltimore & Ohio, the Chicago, Burlington & Quincy, the Chicago & Northwestern, the Chicago & Rock Island, and the Atchison, Topeka & Santa Fe. The organization's name indicated that only managers could belong, and that meant only general managers,

George Pullman had great ambitions for the workers at his company, but his stubborn insistence on controlling their lives led to frustration and distrust.

assistant general managers, and general superintendents. In 1894 the railroads represented by these managers had 41,000 miles of track, 221,000 workers,
$818 million in capital stock, and over $102 million
combined net annual earnings.

Working conditions and wages were major concerns of
the managers. They pooled their information and
shared it among themselves to help deal with demands
for wage increases made by workers. They kept charts
of what each railroad paid each type of worker, and
each road would try to keep their salaries in line with
the others in order to avoid workers' changing jobs for
higher pay. These pay rates were referred to as the
"Chicago scale." Today, these actions would be called
collusion, which is illegal.

For example, the General Managers heard in
February 1893 that there would be a request coming to
increase the wages of switchmen. The switchmen's
union petitioned all of the railroads, because they knew
about the Chicago scale. The association quickly met
and organized three committees to defeat the petition.
They were determined to prove to the workers that
they would not negotiate with unions. Each committee
had only five members. This gave them more discre-
tion and efficiency.

Committee No. 1 recruited and listed switchmen
outside the region who would be willing to be brought
in to substitute if the switchmen went out on strike.

Committee No. 2 was in charge of recording wage rates and making recommendations regarding increase requests. It surprised no one by recommending no increase for the switchmen. Committee No. 3 was to deal with city and county officials in case of a strike, informing them of anything illegal or violent that they thought justified police action. After finding out about this concerted defense on the part of their managers, the switchmen wearily accepted defeat and voted not to strike.

Later that same month, baggage agents asked for a wage increase. Committee No. 2 approved an increase for baggagemasters only; thus a few got raises while the hardest workers got none. This action did not create harmony among the workers, which was exactly what the committee wanted. If the workers could be made to fight among themselves, then their chances of organizing a unified front against the owners were greatly reduced.

This combination of underpaid workers, higher rents, and management determined not to give in to the demands of organized labor created an environment seething with tensions and frustrations. But as long as there were jobs the potential for a major strike only simmered; coming events would bring it to a boil.

Chapter Four

How the Strike Spread

One characteristic of this era was periodic financial panic, when people and lending institutions suddenly began hoarding their money because of fear that an economic calamity was approaching. The irony was that the panic usually caused a depression. In 1893 a deep depression resulted from a series of panics. (It was considered to be the "Great Depression" until the more severe depression of the 1930s.) Millions of jobs were lost and most of those who held onto their jobs had their wages cut.

The Pullman workers did not suffer at the beginning of the depression. The World's Columbian Exposition (also called the Chicago Fair) stimulated work at the Pullman Company because the twenty-seven million visitors needed transportation. People who could afford to come to the Exposition from long distances wanted the comfortable accommodations best provided by the Pullman Palace Cars.

After the Exposition, however, the demand for new cars slowed. The Pullman Company did not need as many employees to build, although some were still needed to repair and refurbish cars in service that were either rented or sold to railroads.

The business conditions of 1893-94 led directly to the Pullman Strike. Although George Pullman made an effort to not lay-off workers, he did cut wages. But most damaging was his refusal to lower rents and fees in his model village. The workers were desperate, caught in a trap of lower wages and high rent and food cost. This combination of forces made a strike almost unavoidable.

A few days after the strike began, Eugene Debs arrived in Pullman. He was unhappy about the Pullman Strike because he did not think it came at a good time. He knew that the high levels of unemployment had created a vast pool of workers desperate for jobs. The company would have no trouble finding the replacement workers that the strikers referred to as "scabs." But by May 16, after he had spoken with many of the strikers, he felt they had a legitimate complaint. Debs expressed his feelings:

> I believe a rich plunderer like Pullman is a greater felon than a poor thief, and it has become no small part of the duty of this organization to strip the mask of

> hypocrisy from the pretended philanthropist and show him to the world as an oppressor of labor....The paternalism of Pullman is the same as the interest of a slave holder in his human chattels.

Reverend William Carwardine of the First Methodist Church of Pullman sided with the strikers and testified poignantly of their dilemma. He published a little book about the strike. He wrote about the relief organization established to get food for families suddenly without income. The first gift to the organization was from the mayor of Chicago's law firm in nearby Kensington. It contributed 25,000 pounds of flour and meat and the free use of a sick-care room. Other provisions followed "from a bottle of ink to a load of flour," said Carwardine, who also noted in his book that strikers and sympathizers wore white ribbons after a suggestion by Eugene Debs.

When Pullman Company supporters opposed to the strike pinned on American flags, some strike supporters added the flag on top of their white ribbon in protest. "The American flag ought to be the best guaranty that an honest day's work should receive an honest day's pay," said Reverend F. Atchison, pastor of the Hyde Park Methodist Episcopal Church and a supporter of the strike.

The Pullman workers hoped that they would receive formal support from the American Railway Union.

Many of them were members. Its scheduled convention began in Chicago on June 12, 1894, just one month after the strike began. Many railway union members visited Pullman and talked with strikers.

On June 21 a special committee of the American Railway Union proposed that if the Pullman Company did not agree to arbitration by June 26, there should be a boycott on handling Pullman cars everywhere. The committee also called for employees of other Pullman factories to strike. The proposal was accepted. Pullman's Vice President Wickes was informed of the union's demands.

The American Railway Union thought that the boycott would result in loss of business and that this economic pressure would force the Pullman Company to arbitrate with the strikers. The tactics were spelled out by Debs in this manner: car inspectors would refuse to inspect Pullman cars; switchmen would refuse to couple them onto trains, and engineers would refuse to move trains forward with Pullman cars on them. If these workers were fired and replaced, then all railroad workers would stop working immediately in support.

On June 26, the boycott deadline, Pullman and Wickes again said there was "nothing to arbitrate." By June 28 about 18,000 workers were on strike. Major roads like the Illinois Central, the Chicago & Northwestern, and the Atchison, Topeka & Santa Fe were seriously affected by the strike in Pullman.

After the intervention of the American Railway Union, the General Managers realized they were no longer dealing with local brotherhoods of switchmen or brakemen, but with a large umbrella organization. The managers were furious that the railroads were being punished when the Pullman Company only did business with passenger railroads, and was not a railroad itself. They thought it intolerable for these workers to prevent the railroads from fulfilling their contracts because of a dispute with Pullman. They voted to discharge any worker who joined the strike and never to rehire him.

After this vote, Committee No. 1 began hiring replacement workers from outside the Chicago region and guaranteed these new workers protection. This was easily done by telegraphing railroad managers who then ran ads in their cities. Soon there were thousands of workers eagerly signing up for the new jobs.

Committee No. 3 set up an office to be open twenty-four hours a day where any manager could report on interference with train movements, violence and the need for police protection. The goal was to create an atmosphere of lawlessness that would prompt the governmental authorities to become involved on management's side. The office made frequent requests for intervention to the police, the sheriff and eventually to the United States marshal.

On July 6, 1894, U.S. troops replaced the strikers who had been guarding the Pullman Plant. The Arcade building was the most expensive and impressive of all the buildings in Pullman, Illinois.

The General Managers also asked for legal advice from the best railroad lawyers. The lawyers told them that for successful prosecution of offenders "action which can be had under the federal laws will be more speedy and efficacious." In other words, the managers needed to find the best pretense to convince federal authorities that they should intervene on management's side.

The most readily available actions that involved federal laws were accusations of interference with the U.S. mail and interstate commerce. These charges could be made through the United States district attorney's office. The General Managers' chief strategy became to turn the struggle between workers and their employers into a battle between workers and the government. Following this strategy, they then withdrew passenger trains from scheduled runs and said railroads would not accept freight since it could not be shipped. This freight included U.S. mail.

On that same day the General Managers' anti-strike manager John Egan announced that the American Railway Union had fought the railroads to a standstill. He said that only federal troops from Fort Sheridan north of Chicago could restore law and quell the strike and boycott.

By July 2 the American Railway Union members realized their plan to bring the railroads to the bargaining table had been foiled, and that the General

Managers were actually trying to increase the delays and inconvenience so the public would clamor for federal intervention. The union had made a mistake by intervening in the strike.

United States Attorney General Richard Olney began receiving complaints about forcible seizures of trains by strikers and other incidents of violence. Square-faced, with stern eyes and drooping mustache, Olney was known for prompt and forceful action. A former railroad lawyer, he was also opposed to the workers going on strike. Olney, President Cleveland, General John Schofield of the Army, and War Secretary Daniel Lamont followed the strike from Washington, D.C. Olney encouraged Cleveland to issue orders to stop the strikers from interfering with the mail.

Debs explained that American Railway Union members were not stopping the mail. They simply wanted the railroads to remove the Pullman cars from trains. The General Managers argued that if trains ran without Pullman cars, the railroads would be guilty of breaking their contracts with the Pullman Company. Therefore, they could not allow the trains to leave without the Pullman cars. This meant that the trains could not run, which resulted in a delay or standstill of the mail on some passenger trains.

The General Managers' plan worked. This argument gave Olney the opening he needed to intervene in the strike. On June 28 he issued telegrams to U.S. district

U.S. Attorney General Richard Olney was eager for federal troops to intervene in the strike to support the railroads.

attorneys that they should arrest any people obstructing mail trains. On June 30 Olney also authorized the swearing-in of deputies by the U.S. marshal. These deputies would ride the mail trains as guards.

On July 1 reports of disturbances in towns outside of Chicago were sent to Washington by both U.S. district attorney Thomas Milchrist and U.S. marshal J.W. Arnold. The next day Olney ordered federal judges in Chicago to issue a restraining order, called an injunction, against Debs and the American Railway Union. This injunction forbade them to encourage, persuade, or threaten railroad workers to abandon their jobs. They were also forbidden to hinder "mail trains, express trains, or other trains, whether freight or passenger, engaged in interstate commerce." The federal government had moved in on the side of Pullman and the General Managers to end the strike.

In 1887 Congress had passed the Interstate Commerce Act. The purpose of the law had been to regulate the rates railroads could charge farmers and other manufacturers to transport their goods. It had been advocated for years by farmers and others who were forced to pay the railroads exorbitant fees. Now Olney used the Interstate Commerce Act to justify the action he took against the strikers because they were restricting trade. In the same way the Sherman Anti-Trust Law of 1890 was intended to slow the growth of the trusts that were stamping out competiton in many

President Grover Cleveland ignored Governor Altgeld's request to allow Illinois officials to deal with the strike. At Attorney General Olney's insistence, Cleveland sent federal troops to Chicago.

industries by setting prices instead of letting the free market system establish what a product or service was worth. Olney argued that the American Railway Union and Pullman strikers had formed an illegal trust, therefore the government had the right to break up the strikers' actions as an illegal act. Ironically, two laws that were passed to control the power of giant business were being used against the workers.

The injunction was personally presented to Debs, and it was printed in all newspapers and posted in public places for all to read. In the July 3 edition of the *New York Times*, the injunction was angrily called a "Gatling gun on paper" and "a veritable dragnet in matter of legal verbiage," but most newspapers agreed with Olney's action.

When U.S. marshal Arnold went to the scene of a disturbance in the Rock Island rail yards at Blue Island near Chicago and read the injunction aloud, he heard "jibes, cheers, and groans" from a crowd of two thousand strike sympathizers. He telegraphed an alarming report to Olney of "a desperate time" and complained of his "inadequate force." Arnold also reported mobs detaching mail cars, overturning freight cars, and controlling rail junctions. His judgment was that it would be "impossible to move trains here without having the Fifteenth Infantry from Fort Sheridan ordered here."

Arnold soon got what he wanted. President Cleveland told General Schofield to move the troops to

This magazine illustration depicts the Army troops in the Chicago Stockyards. The strikers are portrayed as violent and almost out of control.

Chicago. The troops arrived after midnight and found Chicago quiet. No trains were moving. Although the Blue Island riot had been off in a remote southern suburb, the troops were sent not only to Blue Island but to the Chicago Stock Yards. These troop movements were based upon the advice of Marshal Arnold, District Attorney Milchrist and the General Managers' Egan.

Illinois Governor John Altgeld was furious when he heard that federal troops were in Chicago. Neither Cleveland nor Olney had informed Altgeld that Army soldiers were coming. The U.S. Constitution requires that the state legislature or governor must make requests for Army help in their own state. Federal officials are restricted from sending in troops for their own purposes. The fact that President Cleveland had sent in troops without even advising Altgeld and that he would not wait for a request from Illinois authorities was a direct insult to the governor.

Governor Altgeld thought that the Chicago police, the Cook County sheriff, and the Illinois militia had the situation under control. He believed Chicago superintendent of police Michael Brennan, Mayor John Hopkins, and Cook County sheriff Gilbert when they reported their forces were in control. Altgeld had already established a reputation for sending Illinois troops to areas of trouble when requested by sheriffs. In the Pullman Strike, he had responded to requests from the Cairo, Decatur, Danville, and Springfield sheriffs for assistance. There was no need for federal troops.

Altgeld suspected that John Egan and his General Managers' Committee No. 3 were exaggerating incidents and the potential for danger to federal officials and pretending that they desperately needed help that local and state officials could not give. While the railroad managers had reported disorders "bordering on anarchy," investigating local police had found the disturbance to be considerably less violent than the managers had claimed.

Governor Altgeld telegraphed a protest to President Cleveland and Attorney General Olney. He said that newspaper accounts of obstructive incidents "have in some cases been pure fabrications and in others wild exaggerations." Many trains were not moving because the railroads could not get men to operate them. The railroads were saying that mobs were causing the standstill in order to win public sympathy.

Governor Altgeld also stated his belief that Cleveland and Olney had violated the Constitution by sending in troops without his or the Illinois legislature's request:

> To absolutely ignore a local government in matters of this kind, when that government is ready to furnish any assistance needed, and is amply able to enforce the law, not only insults the people of the State...but is in vio-

This painting was done from a photo of federal troops encamped north of the Illinois Central Railroad station near downtown Chicago.

lation of a basic principle of our institutions....Under our Constitution Federal supremacy and local self-government must go hand-in-hand, and to ignore the latter is to do violence to the Constitution.

He requested that all U.S. troops be removed from Chicago. Cleveland replied that he had the legal right to protect the U.S. mails. In reply, Altgeld sent him a lengthy telegram protesting Cleveland's "new" and "capricious" assumption of power. It was of no avail. Cleveland was not going to remove the troops.

The arrival of the troops seemed to feed the hoodlum element in the city. There were already many tramps and petty criminals who had come to Chicago for the Columbian Exposition and had become stranded by the depression of 1893. Restless, cunning, and now excited, they were like a dash of gasoline thrown into a fire. On the evening of July 4, these vagabonds were roaming train tracks in mobs that included teenage boys and even some women and children. The next day, they were pushing over freight cars, setting a few on fire, throwing switches, and stoning trains.

On the night of July 5, a huge fire burned many buildings of the Columbian Exposition in Jackson Park. No suspects were arrested, but strike sympathizers were quickly blamed.

On July 6 another mob started fires in the Illinois Central yards by igniting freight cars. The wind was strong, and the flames spread down the lines of box cars where fire hoses could not reach. The belching red and black mass of destruction roared for several miles before it was stopped. That evening seven hundred cars were also looted and torched in the Panhandle yards in South Chicago near Fiftieth Street. The Illinois militia was dispatched to clear the tracks and restore order.

The mobs continued their destruction on July 7. At the intersection of Loomis and Forty-ninth Streets, a moving train stopped for crew and soldiers to clear an obstruction. A nearby mob of several thousand hurled stones at the crew and soliders. The troops commander ordered a bayonet charge that injured several people. This attack further angered the mob. They then over-turned a flat car, threw more stones, and even fired bullets. After four soldiers were wounded, the commander ordered his men to fire into the crowd. This action finally dispersed the crowd. Four rioters were killed and twenty wounded. This was the climax of the riot in Chicago.

The malicious destruction by lawless rioters dissolved whatever sympathy most people had for the Pullman strike and boycott, although Pullman employees were not among the roving mobs. The Pullman workers had even taken precautions to avoid violence at the onset of the strike by establishing protective guards at the Pullman plant. But they were still blamed, along with boycotting members of the

Illinois militia firing into the mob at Loomis and Forty-ninth Streets in Chicago, July 7, 1894.

American Railway Union, for the violence that the mobs committed.

Newspapers everywhere were filled with the sensational details. Although some reporters wrote of union members trying to persuade the rioters to go home, most of the reports were filled with frightening detail.

Every Chicago resident was increasingly affected by the strike. The city was dependent on shipments of fruit, vegetables, milk, and meat. Thirteen railroads had ceased all movement by July 5, and ten were able to operate only passenger trains. This was not because of the rioters, but because the railroad workers were enacting the boycott they had voted on.

The General Managers knew it was time to make a massive move to kill the strike. They proposed on July 7 that the Chicago police, the Illinois militia, and the federal troops coordinate their efforts. Mayor Hopkins agreed, but said that no one commander could order the other organization's troops. The General Managers brought in their outside trainmen to run the trains under guard.

President Cleveland received many telegrams and letters from the people of Chicago who wanted to restore law and order and to return to business as usual. On July 8 Cleveland issued an Executive Proclamation warning the Chicago mobs to stop the violence and to go home before noon on July 9. If they did not obey this proclamation, they would be treated as public enemies by soldiers.

The rioting in Chicago now ended. Five people had been killed by the Illinois militia, none by federal troops. Sixteen had been seriously injured. The railroads had suffered several hundred thousand dollars in damage. Not a single Pullman car was destroyed because none were in the freight yards where the rioting broke out.

On July 10 the track from the Chicago Stock Yards was cleared, and the Rock Island also resumed operation of suburban passenger trains. By July 13 everything was normal. On July 19 the federal troops were removed. The Illinois militia left gradually and was gone by August 7.

Chapter Five

The Strike Moves Beyond Pullman

When the American Railway Union members voted on June 21, 1894 to boycott the handling of Pullman cars, they started a chain reaction. Soon workers in other Western states began boycotting and striking also. In St. Louis, workers on the Missouri Pacific filed notice that they would not handle Pullman cars. When a switchman then refused to move a Pullman, he was fired. His co-union members requested his rehiring. When the request was rejected, all union members went out on strike.

There were also cases where the workers removed the Pullman cars from the line, but railroad managers refused to let trains leave. The Atchison, Topeka & Santa Fe Railroad was in serious financial trouble. Wages were several months overdue. This had already created tension among the workers, and the men showed their frustration by sidetracking Pullman cars. On July 1 in Trinidad, Colorado, a mob disarmed the deputy marshals.

The American Railway Union knew the tensions created by the workers' refusing to move Pullman cars and the railroads' refusals to move trains without the cars attached could easily erupt into violence. In an effort to forestall this, they applied for a federal injunction on July 4 to force the Union Pacific to operate trains without Pullman cars. The injunction was denied.

After receiving news of the problems in Colorado, President Cleveland ordered out the federal troops from Fort Logan near Denver. After pausing to fix cut telegraph wires in Pueblo, the soldiers arrived in Trinidad on July 4. Forty-eight men were arrested and sent to Denver to be tried for contempt of court.

At Raton, New Mexico, when a strike ensued, passengers stayed on their disconnected Pullman cars in the yards with nowhere to go. The station manager found money to buy meals for them. Three hundred local coal miners came to Raton in sympathy with the strikers. The local sheriff warned the federal marshal that there would be real trouble if he tried to impose his will on the workers.

On the night of July 3, rioters in Raton released the brakes on sixteen boxcars. The cars roared down the steep grade, crashed into the yards, and blocked them. The next evening, against the sheriff's advice, federal troops arrived and the miners vanished. The strikers in Raton returned to work.

A contemporary magazine illustration of the burning of six hundred freight cars on the evening of July 6, 1894, in the Panhandle yards in South Chicago.

In California, both the general public and the majority of newspapers supported the strike and boycott. For them the Southern Pacific Railroad was a monopoly of giant proportions, not only controlling freight rates but spreading into ship lines, harbor connections, and even streetcars. Californians could not understand why the Sherman Anti-Trust Law was not applied to the Southern Pacific, while it was used against the Pullman strikers and American Railway Union boycotters.

The pro-strike sympathy was so strong that in some places marshals had trouble finding men to restore order. Some state militiamen said they would not charge or fire at crowds of civilians. In Los Angeles, the boycott proceeded peacefully and effectively with no trains moving.

Sacramento was the hottest center of pro-union workers. Three-fourths of the 2500 railroad workers went on strike, and they were joined by another five hundred workers from surrounding towns. When the U.S. marshal ordered a mail train made up, the workers disconnected the Pullman cars.

These workers resisted when the deputies tried to arrest them. Frightened, the marshal wired the governor for state troops. When the troops arrived, some of them refused to charge or fire upon the strikers. Most of the troops also lived in California. Their reluctance to punish the strikers shows how angry the people of California were about the Southern Pacific monopoly in their state.

Now President Cleveland and Attorney General Olney decided that federal troops were necessary not only to protect the mails and interstate commerce, but to also keep the railroads open for the military. The rationale for this decision was based upon the government's help financing the construction of the Central Pacific Railroad (now owned by the Southern Pacific) in the 1860s. Part of the railroad's obligation, in return for the federal financial assistance, was to carry U.S. troops when necessary for defense. This was such a time, according to Cleveland and Olney, which meant they could order in more force in the name of national security.

On July 11 five hundred Army soldiers came up the Sacramento River by boat. The next day they drove away crowds in the railroad yards without firing a shot. Several soldiers were killed, though, when a train they were guarding enroute to San Francisco was derailed by sabotage. One striker was later killed in the Sacramento yards when soldiers fired upon a crowd pelting them with stones.

By July 13 the Central Pacific line from Ogden to San Francisco was in operation. Although trouble had been anticipated in Oakland, where women were rolling bandages and a temporary hospital had been organized, no violence occurred.

In Nebraska, Wyoming, and Utah, there was much sympathy for the strikers. In Wyoming, where the population along the railroad was largely railroad workers, there were few people who would not benefit from a successful strike. In Rawlins, Wyoming, the U.S. marshal and his deputies were ordered to leave town, but when the federal troops arrived to guard the trains, there was no resistance. By July 16 trains were moving from Omaha to San Francisco.

Running from St. Paul, Minnesota, to Seattle, Washington, the Northern Pacific was another railroad that had been built with government loans. It had agreed to transport both military and mail. On June 26 American Railway Union members began boycotting it. The action soon spread, accompanied by some vandalism, including the burning of a bridge.

On July 3 the Army commander of the Dakotas wired that he had received no mail since June 25. Attorney General Olney ordered troops to accompany trains along the entire Northern Pacific route starting July 6. The first trains witnessed angry but non-violent demonstrations from strikers enroute.

Oklahoma, though not yet a state in 1894, witnessed violence against the Rock Island Railroad. Trains were derailed and one bridge was blown up as a train passed over it. Marshals and deputies proved ineffective and the governor called for federal troops on July 12.

In Iowa, especially Sioux City and Dubuque, after switches were thrown at junctions to halt trains, the governors called out the state militia.

From the East to Chicago, trains had to follow the southern coast of Lake Michigan through the city of Hammond, Indiana. Hammond sat at the junction of many railroads which employed members of the American Railway Union. These members were actively boycotting. They stopped trains and uncoupled the Pullman cars as they passed through to Chicago. The governor of Indiana wanted no state troops sent because the boycott was being conducted peacefully.

When the U.S. marshal arrested some union officials in Hammond, the mood changed. Large mobs formed with "recruits" drawn from the ranks of the hooligans and rioters of Chicago. This mob created chaos by attacking replacement trainmen, derailing engines and cars, and taking over a Western Union telegraph office. By July 7 train traffic had completely stopped.

Though advised by his district attorney on July 8 to call for federal troops, Governor Mathews of Indiana was like Governor Altgeld of Illinois. He stuck by his original decision and insisted the Indiana militia could handle the rioters.

Dismayed, Olney ordered in federal troops anyway. Some of these men, moving up and down the tracks, fired at anything even slightly suspicious. They killed a carpenter who was looking for his lost son. This created further resentment in Hammond because the carpenter was well known and liked.

The boycott did not move further east of Hammond despite rallies of support in cities like Boston and New York. There were few members of the American Railway Union in the East where Wagner and Monarch sleeping cars were primarily used instead of Pullman cars.

But people felt some effects nevertheless. According to New York newspapers, food prices soared for whatever goods were shipped in from the West. Peaches that were one dollar per box cost three dollars and sixty cents on July 5. Chicken went up five cents a pound during the strike.

Another reason the boycott failed to move to the East was that the individual railway brotherhoods mistrusted and feared the American Railway Union. They did not want to become part of a large industrial union. They wanted to bargain in smaller groups as locomotive engineers, firemen, switchmen, trainmen, or conductors. A sympathetic strike was preposterous to them. Some Eastern railroad workers even agreed with the General Managers' argument that the railroads had made contracts with the Pullman Company and should not let the trains move without those Pullman cars on them.

The lack of sympathy was also created by the

greater unemployment among Eastern railroad workers with about one-third out of work. The depression of
1893 had taken a terrible toll. Many of these men of
the East were eager to get work and many were willing to replace strikers.

Chapter Six

Debs and the Law

Despite the setback caused by the federal intervention on the side of the General Managers, Eugene Debs continued to think the strikers and boycotters would win. The strikers' cause was also weakened when some of the Pullman plants did not join the strike. Pullman repair shops in Wilmington, Delaware had refused unionization and never ceased operation. The repair shops in Ludlow, Kentucky and St. Louis, Missouri that had struck on June 25 had been kept in operation with replacement workers.

Debs, always optimistic, was heartened by all the shut-downs in the West even as the injunction and troop orders were carried out. His telegrams still resounded with victory hopes on July 16:

> We have assurance that within 48 hours every labor organization will come to our rescue. The tide is on and the men are acquitting themselves like heroes. Here and there one weakens, but our cause is strengthened by others going out in their places.

By July 18 the Pullman Company posted notice that the plant would open. Strikers could reapply for their jobs and would be rehired only if they renounced their membership in the American Railway Union. The workers had to accept their old wage and house rental rates in the town of Pullman.

Debs had been consulting with constitutional lawyers in Chicago during the strike and was convinced that he was acting within the law as long as he did not advocate violence, which he hated. However, he and union members were blamed for the violence that did break out. Because of this violence U.S. district attorney Thomas Milchrist in Chicago decided to arrest Debs. Attorney General Olney in Washington agreed with this decision.

During the second week of July, a grand jury in Chicago was ordered to examine evidence against Eugene Debs. If it found sufficient evidence that Debs had violated the July 2 injunction, then he would be arrested and tried for conspiracy to disrupt the mails.

The jury was given some of Debs' telegram copies which had been subpoenaed from Western Union. No calls to violence were found, but the urgings to support the boycott seemed to indicate conspiracy, defined by Judge Peter Grosscup as "an agreement on the part of two or more individuals to stop trains unlawfully [that] would have the effect of halting mail trains and interstate commerce."

On July 10 Debs and his three American Railway Union officers were indicted by the grand jury and arrested for the first time. They were charged with conspiracy to obstruct the U.S. mails. It took several hours to raise the bail of $10,000. After paying the bail, each was allowed to go free until their trial began in seven days.

On July 17 Debs and his colleagues were arrested for a second charge: contempt of the court's July 2 injunction by multiple and willful violations. This time Debs refused to pay the bail money. He explained, "The poor striker who is arrested would be thrown in jail. We are no better than he."

The hearing began on July 23. Debs' lawyers argued that the contempt charges and the conspiracy charges were for the same actions. Because it is illegal to try a person twice for the same offense, they argued to have the contempt charge dropped.

After the judge ruled in disagreement, Debs' lawyers asked for a jury trial in a criminal court. They felt that a decision in an equity court by a judge only would be prejudiced against Debs and the American Railway Union. This request was also denied.

In the contempt trial that followed, the prosecuting lawyers argued that the government has the right to remove a "public nuisance." It said that a railroad was one kind of a public highway, and since courts could remove obstacles on roads, they could do the same on rails. By uniting workers to withdraw service from an interstate railroad, the union leaders had obstructed travel flow. According to this reasoning, the workers and Debs were guilty of being a public nuisance and were thus in contempt of the injunction.

On December 14 the judge declared Debs and his co-defendants guilty of contempt. Debs was sentenced to six months in prison, the three other men to three months each. They began serving their sentences on January 8, 1895, in the Woodstock jail because the Cook County jail in Chicago was full.

Debs' lawyers appealed to the United States Supreme Court. They argued that the contempt trial had been conducted in the wrong court and was therefore unconstitutional. They argued that refusal to work for a railroad is not a crime and that the interference with interstate commerce and mail delivery was incidental to the strike, not directly intended by it. They argued also that to be charged for a crime, defendants have the right to be tried in a criminal court and receive a trial by jury. The lawyers pointed out that Debs and his men had not received these rights in their equity court trial by a judge.

Attorney General Richard Olney argued against Debs before the Supreme Court. He said the union officials were no more blameless than a man holding a lighted match near gunpowder. Olney went on to say that the government is like a trustee and it must protect the property that is committed to its care.

Famous lawyer Clarence Darrow, who years later argued the Scopes "Monkey Trial" in Tennessee, was Debs' defense attorney in his conspiracy tiral.

On May 27, 1895 the Supreme Court unanimously agreed with Olney. This decision established an important principle for strong federal power. The Supreme Court's decision stated that the federal government has the power to prevent interference with the mail and interstate commerce because the Constitution gives that same Federal government the power to control the postal system and to make laws regarding interstate commerce. It also decided that a court of equity may be used by the government to rule about public nuisances. This Supreme Court decision came to be known as the Debs Decision or *In re Debs*, Latin for "about the Debs matter."

Having been sentenced for contempt and having lost the appeal to the Supreme Court, Debs was next tried for conspiracy, along with twenty other American Railway Union officials. This trial was heard by a jury in a criminal court with Judge Grosscup presiding. It began on January 24, 1895. Debs was brought in every day from the Woodstock jail fifty miles away.

The defendants denied that they had entered into a conspiracy to paralyze the railroads. They claimed they were not in conspiracy against the injunction because they had advised workers to peacefully and lawfully stop work. Their actions had been motivated only by grievances with the Pullman Company and the railroads that carried Pullman cars. In fact, they insisted the railroads and the Pullman Company were partnered

Eugene Debs in his sixties. After the Pullman Strike he ran for president of the United States as a Socialist Party candidate four times.

in a conspiracy to reduce wages and prevent the American Railway Union members from receiving arbitration.

Lawyers Clarence Darrow and Stephen Strong Gregory defended Debs. Darrow began the defense by charging that the prosecuting attorney was a "puppet in the hands of the great railroad corporations in this persecution, not prosecution." He saw this not just as a trial that might result in two years imprisonment and a $10,000 fine, but also as a case that could safeguard or endanger the rights of labor.

Darrow argued that the General Managers were the ones guilty of obstructing the United States mails. They wanted to use public inconvenience of interrupted mail service as the club to beat back better conditions for workingmen and women. He produced the minutes of a General Managers' Association meeting as evidence of conspiracy to reduce wages.

Debs was the chief witness at his own trial. He presented the history and goals of the American Railway Union. He testified that he believed in strict obedience to the law and that he condemned all violence.

Something strange then happened. One of the jury members became ill and left. The judge ruled that adding a replacement at this time would probably not be legal. Darrow argued against this because he sensed that the jury was eleven to one to acquit Debs. He was probably right, for the district attorney a year later entered in the records *"nolle prosequi,"* the legal term from Latin meaning "unwilling to prosecute." This action denied Debs his right to be found not guilty by jury, which would have greatly raised his prestige.

While Debs served the rest of his jail term for the earlier contempt conviction, he read and thought about economic systems. During this period he committed himself to socialism and to the betterment of life for workers in a democracy.

Upon his release from Woodstock, he was greeted as a hero. In following years he ran four times for the United States presidency as nominee of the Socialist Party of America.

When George Pullman died suddenly of a heart attack in 1897, Eugene Debs commented only, "Peace be to his ashes. Mr. Pullman would not arbitrate when he had 'nothing to arbitrate.' He is on an equality with toilers now."

Chapter Seven

The United States Strike Commission

In 1888, six years before the Pullman Strike, Congress passed the Arbitration Act. This legislation guaranteed that Congress would provide mediators to arbitrate conflicts between groups that asked for it. It also agreed to set up fact-finding commissions for labor-management disputes if such a commission were requested by a governor or the U.S. president.

On July 26, 1894, President Cleveland took advantage of this act to appoint three chairmen to inquire into the recent controversies between the Illinois Central and Rock Island railroads and their employees. He instructed the commission to "hear all persons interested therein who may come before it." Carroll D. Wright, United States Commissioner of Labor, was assigned to the commission. Wright was a distinguished statistician from New Jersey and had organized the Bureau of Labor Statistics to provide objective research on labor problems. Nicholas E. Worthington, a lawyer and former congressman from Illinois, and John D. Kernan from New York were chosen as the other chairmen.

The Pullman Strike hearings began on August 15, 1894 in the Chicago post office and lasted for two weeks. The commission spent another day in Washington, D. C. on September 26. Any citizen or organization who wished to testify could do so. If they could not be present, they could send in their testimony in writing. One hundred and nine witnesses were heard by the three commissioners, who followed up the testimonies with questions.

After hearing all the witnesses, the three men carefully prepared their report. It was fifty-four pages full of information called the *Report on the Chicago Strike of June-July, 1894*. The recorded testimony of witnesses was included in an additional 681 pages called an appendix.

According to recorded testimony, the railroads lost $685,308 in destroyed property during the strike. They lost about $4 million in business. Pullman strikers lost $350,000 in wages and striking railroad workers about $1.4 million, with many employees "still adrift and losing wages." The money lost from the paralysis of the Chicago distribution center was "very great" and "widely distributed."

Twelve people had been fatally shot during the course of the strike, 515 arrested by police for murder, arson, burglary, assault, and riot. Seventy-one were arrested for obstruction of U.S. mails or conspiracy to restrain interstate trade.

The report noted the numbers of troops and protection forces present in Chicago during the strike:

U.S. troops July 3-10	1936
Illinois militia July 6-11	4000
Extra deputy marshals	5000
Chicago police force	3000

The commissioners went on to discuss other aspects of the strike that could not be so easily quantified. These elements that needed to be "thoroughly understood by the people and to be wisely and prudently treated by the government" were: 1) the eagerness of laborers to strike; 2) the determination by railroad management to crush the strike rather than look for a peaceful solution; 3) the occasion to burn, loot, and murder which a strike provides for disreputable persons not connected with the strike; 4) the changing of hardworking, law-abiding people into idlers and lawbreakers; 5) the suffering brought to many innocent families; and 6) the changing of railroad yards, stations, and markets into dangerous, armed camps.

The commission's report also presented a section of facts about the Pullman Palace Car Company, the American Railway Union, and the General Managers' Association. Here the commissioners stated that they did not favor an industrial union like the American Railway Union because the complexity of its members' different training, skills, conditions, and pride tended to defeat rather than assist their common goals. They disliked that people who built railway cars were united with those who operated the trains: "This mistake led the union into a strike purely sympathetic and aided to bring upon it a crushing and demoralizing defeat."

The commissioners condemned the General Managers' Association as illegal. They called it "an illustration of the persistent and shrewdly devised plans of corporations to overreach...and usurp powers and rights." By pooling and charting their wage scales, they were fixing wages. The commissioners stated that it is "rank injustice" for them to do so and not to allow the workers to do the same through a union.

The loss of business to the Pullman Company following the depression of 1893 was acknowledged as a cause for the layoffs and cut in pay that Pullman had forced upon his workers. But the commissioners said the employees were unfairly made to bear the brunt of the loss. While workers' wages fell an average of twenty-five percent, no salaries of officers, managers, or superintendents were lowered. Though the Pullman Company showed evidence that it sustained losses in order to keep workers employed, the commissioners thought otherwise:

> The evidence shows that it sought to keep running mainly for its own benefit as a manufacturer, that its plant might not rust, that its competitors might not invade its

STUPIDITY and GREED

AN IMPENDING DOWNFALL.

—*Ram's Horn.*

This cartoon captured most people's attitude toward the Pullman Strike.
To most Americans both sides behaved foolishly.

territory, that it might keep its cars in repair, that it might be ready for resumption when business revived with a live plant and competent help, and that its revenue from its tenements might continue.

The commission's report summarized the events leading to the Pullman workers' strike and the American Railway Union boycott. The subsequent strike by railroad employees was defined as a sympathetic one, with no grievances presented against railroads: "Throughout the strike, the strife was simply over handling Pullman cars, the men being ready to do their duty otherwise." This sympathy was promoted by the fear felt by many from former wage reductions, blacklisting and the growing power of the General Managers' Association.

It was found that in some cases, the strikers had broken their contracts with the railroads, most notably the Illinois Central, and had justified their actions as "balancing wrongs." When union agents urged them on, disorders had flamed out of control.

The commissioners found that both the Pullman Company and the General Managers' Association had repeatedly turned down proposals for arbitration or peaceful settlement. The General Managers' Association had also set up headquarters to hire replacement workers, give information to the press, complain to the police, and maintain communications with all railroads.

sted; they have a blacklist there and I have one of them in my pocket, imilar to the one sent out to different railroad companies.

36 (Commissioner WRIGHT). Will you produce it. and submit it as art of your testimony?—Ans. Yes, sir; the blacklist that was made ut in December is as follows:

PULLMAN, ILL., *December 23, 1893.*

o all foremen:

In connection with the recent trouble we have had with steam fitters, both in the onstruction and repair departments, I give below the names of the men who have ift our employ, and I hereby instruct that none of these men be employed in these orks.

CONSTRUCTION DEPARTMENT.

o. 1703. Joseph Cohan.
1705. Frank McKevilt.
1706. William O'Meara.
1707. James H. Matthews.
1711. Edward Sweeney.
1715. John Guthardt.
1721. Martin Tracey.
1720. Tice Mastenbrook.
1722. Charles G. Duffy.
1740. Frank Vincent.
1743. Michael McNulty.
1753. William H. Danaher.

No. 1764. Edward M. Barrett.
4500. Jacob Stockman.
4516. Robert Goebbels.
4563. James A. Brown.
4564. Louis Moss.
4565. Thomas Hamilton.
Daniel J. McCarthy (*a*).
John A. Smith (*a*).
Frank Pohl (*a*).
Ambrose J. Hough (*a*).
George Elwell (*a*).

REPAIR DEPARTMENT.

o. 6976. Frank Engel, steam fitter.
6977. B. Jones, steam fitter.
6978. Thomas Johnston, steam fitter.
6980. Wm. J. Connell. steam fitter.
6982. August Berghofer, helper.
6983. Chas. R. McGinnis, steam fitter.
6985. C. Patton, steam fitter.
6985. P. McCaffrey, steam fitter.
6988. Martin Craig, steam fitter.

No. 6990. J. C. Warburton, steam fitter.
6995. B. O. Gara. steam fitter.
7002. Josh. Jones, helper.
7007. William Mack, helper.
7015. Mike Carroll, helper.
7016. Frank Oberreich, helper.
7035. Dave Burrows, helper.
7024. M. Cunningham, helper.
7025. James Payne, helper.

H. MIDDLETON, *Manager.*

37 (Commissioner KERNAN). Where did you get this list?—Ans. It as given to me after the strike. Of course I do not want to name the aan, but it came from the company's office, and it was presented to me y one of the friends of one of the clerks.

38 (Commissioner KERNAN). Have you any objection to stating who he clerk was?—Ans. I do not want to, for he would lose his position.

39 (Commissioner WRIGHT). Have you suffered from this blacklist-ig method at Pullman?—Ans. I have not yet myself, but I am con-inced that I shall never be able to get a job in the railway service gain.

This listing of union workers who were blacklisted at Pullman was taken from the Strike Commission's report.

It was found that the association also armed and paid 3,600 guards whom they got the U.S. marshal to deputize. Thus, these men were taking orders from the railroads but exercising the power of the United States.

The report confirmed that Chicago, "the center of an activity and growth unprecedented in history," had attracted "shiftless adventurers and criminals" who had become a "lawless element" when they were stranded after the Columbian Exposition and the depression of 1893. It also referred to "objectionable foreigners, who are being precipitated on us by unrestricted immigration." This population saw the strike as "an opportunity...to burn and plunder" and was the component of "the mobs that took possession of railroad yards, tracks, and crossings...that stoned, tipped over, burned, and destroyed cars and stole their contents."

Railroad strikers were mainly responsible for "the spiking and misplacing of switches, removing rails, crippling of interlocking systems, the detaching, side tracking, and derailing of cars and engines, placing of coupling pins in engine machinery, blockading tracks with cars, and attempts to detach and run in mail cars."

In their conclusion the commissioners wrote, "Many impartial observers are reaching the view that much of the real responsibility for these disorders rests with the people themselves and with the Government for not adequately controlling monopolies and corporations, and for failing to reasonably protect the rights of labor and redress its wrongs."

They also abhorred striking as a means of remedy. "It is encouraging to find general concurrence, even among labor leaders, in condemning strikes, boycotts, and lockouts as barbarisms unfit for the intelligence of this age, and as, economically considered, very injurious and destructive forces."

Included in their conclusion, the commissioners made three major recommendations to be presented to President Cleveland and Congress in November, 1894:

1. A permanent U.S. Strike Commission should be created to investigate disputes between railroads and their employees and to make recommendations that the railroads must obey. Both railroads and incorporated national trade unions involved shall send elected representatives to be temporary members during their controversy.

2. The individual states should provide a) a system of arbitration like the one already in Massachusetts and b) legal standing to labor organizations. Contracts requiring workers not to join a labor organization or to leave them as a condition of employment should be illegal.

3. Employers should recognize labor organizations. They should "come in closer touch with labor and recognize that, while the interests of labor and capital are not identical, they are reciprocal." Wages should be raised when economic conditions allow, and when they are reduced, the reasons should be given. Employers should consider employees as essential as money to business success, and should consult with them when appropriate.

The 681 pages of printed testimony provide fascinating reading. The format is like a play script, which gives the reader a feeling of being present at the hearing. Commissioners Wright, Kernan, and Worthington ask questions like good lawyers or police officers, careful to distinguish between fact and hearsay, addressing all witnesses with respect and dignity.

The reader feels the desperation of Pullman employees like Thomas Heathcoate (car builder), Jennie Curtis (seamstress), Theodore Rhodie (painter), or Mary Alice Wood (electrical department worker) as they describe the details of their humiliating poverty. At other times the reader feels the frightening presence of the mobs along the tracks in south Chicago.

The appendix included passages from one reporter for the *Chicago Record* who had ridden as far as Hammond, Indiana, on Sunday, July 8. There he encountered a mob that had turned back several passenger trains. "A big, rough-looking fellow whom the people called 'Pat' led the mob down and they threw two ropes over the top of the Pullman car" standing isolated on the track. Pulling in unison, the men rocked to overturn the car, while women and children gathered to watch. Just as the car was about to go over, a caboose and locomotive arrived with U.S. troops aboard. The troops fired without warning into the crowd. Everyone scattered and hid behind box cars, but one man was killed. The reporter did not know this was the innocent carpenter looking for his son.

Another reporter witnessed the U.S. marshal's reading of President Cleveland's injunction to a group of men in the Rock Island yards. These men did not look like railroad workers, but like tough brickyard workers. They started jeering, "To hell with the President! To hell with the court and injunctions!" A Rock Island official then told them that if they laid hands on any cars, they could be arrested. "That started them all crying and jeering again, and then it was that several American Railway Union men climbed up on the back platform and told the men they must stop the hooting and yelling; that the injunction meant business, and they must get away, and in fifteen or twenty minutes the mob, as it was called, dispersed."

When asked by Commissioner Kernan how he knew the men urging compliance were union officials, the reporter replied, "Because they told me they belonged to the union, and two or three of them had little white buttons with A.R.U. on them."

There was also testimony about the town of Pullman and the extent to which it was indeed "model." Jane Addams, the superintendent of the Hull House in Chicago, was active in making life better for the poor and had visited Pullman at the request of the Civic Federation. She had been asked to determine the attitude towards arbitration for wages and rent. Her impression was that room rentals were about twenty-five percent higher in Pullman for comparable places in Chicago. She did not go into further investigation because the Pullman officials, although very courteous, "insisted there was nothing to arbitrate."

Chapter Eight

The Pullman Strike's Role in U.S. History

The Pullman Strike happened over one hundred years ago. The world has changed a great deal in the intervening decades. What impact did the strike have on the lives of Americans? What can we learn from it today? Historians and legal scholars have thought and written about it, and they are not always in agreement.

Few happenings have sparked such opposite responses. Mayors, governors, the attorney general, and the president of the United States not only participated in the action but also represented very different perceptions. Newspaper reporting at the time was usually strongly on one side or the other. One historian wrote, "It seemed as if the Pullman boycott split the nation into warring camps, and raised the cries of government by injunction and of anarchy, cries which continued long after the fight ended."

This chapter will focus on seven of the issues involved in the strike and then conclude with the two opposing interpretations.

1. Individual vs. Collective Bargaining

George Pullman refused to "bargain," to accept arbitration with the elected representatives of his employees about their conditions and wages. He and Vice President Thomas Wickes argued that it deprived the worker of his individual liberty to be represented by a union man, even when the individual worker had voted for that fellow worker to speak for him. Pullman and Wickes said they were always willing to listen to any one worker who made an appointment with them. Obviously the workers did not agree that this was always possible—or effective.

Collective bargaining had been first developed in England earlier in the nineteenth century. In the Strike Report the commissioners said the Pullman Company was "behind the age" in denying to labor organizations a "place or necessity in Pullman." Forty years after the Pullman Strike, the National Labor Relations Act of 1935 (also called the Wagner Act) established the right of workers to collective bargaining.

A researcher, Paul K. Edwards, who collected and analyzed facts about strikes in the U.S. from 1881-1981, reports that the most important factors in creating a strike are unemployment and price changes. He concludes that the most important peacemaker in "the unremitting struggle between workers and employers for control of the workplace" in the U.S. is "the establishment of collective bargaining on a wide scale."

2. The Model Town

The model town of Pullman was probably doomed from the beginning because its rentals were not competitively priced with comparable properties in nearby suburbs, and because George Pullman would not relinquish his control. Pullman also would not adjust rates when times were bad because he had determined that the rentals must bring in a profit—ideally five to six percent. The average was about three percent for him at the time of the strike, and he was determined not to back down.

Shortly after the strike ended, the attorney general of Illinois initiated court procedures to end the charter of the model town for violation of corporate rights. In other words, the Pullman Palace Car Company was authorized to build, lease, and sell railway cars but not to acquire real estate holdings or to establish and manage a town. Pullman officials argued that they had been counseled otherwise, and they had not been challenged for fifteen years. They felt that Governor Altgeld wanted to please labor organizations and was making the Pullman Company a victim to do so. They appealed the decision against Pullman to the Illinois Supreme Court in October, 1898. The high court's decision was that a town with all the property owned by a corporation was "opposed to good public policy and incompatible with the theory and spirit of our institutions." Pullman was ordered to sell within five years all property not necessary to manufacturing train cars.

Today the former town of Pullman is a part of Chicago.

3. Industrial Unionism

Unions were first formed to unite workers in a particular craft or skill. There were also unions for locomotive engineers, firemen, brakemen, trainmen, baggage handlers, and others.

The American Railway Union was an industrial union that accepted all kinds of workers from the least to the most skilled. This type of union is sometimes referred to as a vertical union.

The Strike Commission felt that such unions were "not wise," and that the American Railway Union was "a mistake" that exemplified their point. Covering so broad a range of work was certain to create "an infinite variety of conflicting positions." The "complex character, nationalities, habits, and requirements" make such union "a doubtful experiment" at best.

The Pullman Strike eventually destroyed the American Railway Union. Later, in 1905 Eugene Debs helped establish the Industrial Workers of the World, which accepted everyone regardless of skill, race, sex, or creed, ranging from migrant agricultural workers to coal miners.

Two other large industrial unions, the American Federation of Labor (successor to the Knights of Labor) and the Congress of Industrial Organizations had various ways of categorizing their local unions. In 1955 these two giants merged into the AFL-CIO. In 1981 the United Auto Workers joined this umbrella organization as did the Teamsters in 1988. Now unions such as the Service Employees International are attempting to organize workers in service industries and public service.

Industrial unions did not die out after the Pullman Strike. They continued to grow and reached peak power in the first half of the twentieth century. By 1960 thirty-three percent of all American workers belonged to unions. Union membership has been in steep decline since then. In 1990 only sixteen percent of U.S. workers were unionized.

4. Boycotting

There are different kinds of boycotting. Most people think of boycotting as refusing to buy the product of a company with whose policies they disagree, in the hope that the company will change in order to increase financial success.

There are more complicated boycotts, too. The American Railway Union workers boycotted the handling of Pullman cars in order to support the six week-old strike of the Pullman employees. The refusal to handle the Pullman cars resulted in firings and work stoppage, and soon everybody referred to the whole business as a strike or the Chicago Strike.

The Strike Commission condemned strikes and boycotts both as "barbarisms unfit for the intelligence of this age." The Taft-Hartley Act of 1947 and the Landrum-Griffin Act of 1959 prohibited strikes in the aid of a boycott.

Voluntary boycotts are still practiced, though their effectiveness is increasingly questioned if the scale is a large one. In the late 1960s and early 1970s the United Farm Workers urged people not to buy green grapes, so migrant agricultural workers could receive better pay. In the 1970s many liberal organizations boycotted holding conventions in states that had not passed the Equal Rights Amendment. In the 1980s the boycott against South African businesses was widely urged in the United States as a protest against apartheid.

5. Right Of A Public Utility To Strike

Public utilities generally indicates the industries that provide consumers with necessities such as water, gas, electricity, telephone, and transportation. In many nations the public utilities are owned by the state, but in the United States they are frequently privately owned but regulated by laws and commissions with regard to rates, schedules, safety, and profits. Some states require arbitration for disputes. Thus, public utility strikes do not often happen in the U.S.

6. Arbitration

The Strike Commission's recommendations showed the importance of arbitration. It wanted the establishment of a permanent strike commission to compel industries to obey its decisions until the time these could be ruled on by arbitration or legal appeals. The National Labor Relations Board (NLRB) set up by the Wagner Act of 1935 seeks to fulfill what the commissioners had in mind.

In some countries like New Zealand, Canada, Australia, and England, arbitration can be ordered by the government. In the United States, the government must persuade the parties to accept arbitration. The American Arbitration Association formed in 1926 now has 7000 members who can be called to help settle labor disputes.

7. Federal Intervention

Since the beginning of our country, people have disagreed about the relationship between state and federal powers. Such disagreements were a major cause of the Civil War, which ended only twenty-nine years before the Pullman Strike.

Governor Altgeld of Illinois and the governors of Indiana, Colorado, Kansas, Missouri, Oregon, Idaho, and Texas felt the federal government had wrongly intervened in state matters. They protested to Cleveland and Olney. Altgeld argued: "Under this procedure a federal judge sitting in a rear room can on motion of some corporation lawyer issue a ukase which he calls an injunction forbidding anything he chooses to and which the law does not forbid."

Altgeld said that after the injunction against Debs and the American Railway Union, the federal judge became "at once a legislator, court, and executioner." Debs was tried in a court of equity and received his sentence not from a jury but from the federal judge.

The Supreme Court ruled to the contrary. It said the equity court was the proper place for judgment, because the federal government has the constitutional power to remove obstructions to interstate commerce and the U.S. mails. "If emergency arises," the Court continued, "the army of the Nation, and all its militia, are at the service of the Nation to compel obedience to its laws." The injunction did not forbid the workers to quit work; its purpose had been to remove obstructions from the rails on which interstate commerce and the mails traveled:

> We have given to this case the most careful and anxious attention, for we realize that it touches closely questions of supreme importance....We hold that the government of the United States is one having jurisdiction over every foot of soil within its territory, and acting directly upon each citizen; that while it is a government of enumerated powers, it has within the limits of those powers all the attributes of sovereignty....

Did this decision lead to "government by injunction" as Altgeld and labor leaders feared? In the years that followed, employers were often granted injunctions against striking or boycotting workers. But then the workers got legal gains, too. Decisions and laws were rather like a see-saw going up and down, with workers and owners each trying to get the favorable balance.

In 1932 the Federal Anti-Injunction Act restricted federal injunctions against workers. In 1947 the Taft-Hartley Act restored some injunction powers to the courts. In 1959 the Labor-Management Reporting and Disclosure Act allowed injunctions to promote higher ethical standards within unions.

Injunctions have been used in more recent times in other areas, such as civil rights legislation. Injunctions, for example, have enforced racial desegregation of schools since the 1970s.

8. Later Interpretations of Federal Intervention and the Debs Case

President Cleveland's use of the Army in Illinois without the governor's request surprised people. Cleveland was a Democrat, and at that time Democratic Party publicly championed states' rights against the power of the federal government. It was the party most opposed to the growth of federal power. But Olney argued that "the soil of Illinois is the soil of the United States" and that the notion of any state's superiority over the United States "has become practically extinct with the close of the Civil War."

One source of controversy was the fact that President Grover Cleveland, Attorney-General Richard Olney, and Judge Peter Grosscup had all been connected with railroads in their private law practices. Olney in particular was known as a railroad lawyer. But most lawyers of this era who had reached Olney's high position had represented railroads in the course of their careers, including Abraham Lincoln. A legal scholar Willard King took issue with some historians' accusations that they were corrupt. Grover Cleveland was "a man of immense courage and determination," he said, and Judge Grosscup's biography in the *Dictionary of American Biography* reflects an excellent reputation.

King also said that Debs' notion of violence was very limited. Although he was a very kind man who would not hurt a fly, "violence meant assaulting and beating people." For Debs it did not include property damage. Spiking switches, derailing trains, tipping over cars, and burning contents were encouraged by telegrams from Debs that read, "Knock it to them as hard as possible," and "Pay no attention to injunction orders."

Nor did Debs lack superb legal counsel, King pointed out. Several prominent attorneys represented him at his contempt trial, the Supreme Court appeal, and the conspiracy trial, including Lyman Trumbull (who wrote the 13th Amendment to the Constitution,)

Clarence Darrow, and Stephen Strong Gregory (later President of the American Bar Association.)

The Supreme Court unanimously judged that Olney's argument was constitutional. This Supreme Court was a fair and good one, said King; its members were "the staunchest guardians of civil rights that the Court has ever had," and included a Lincoln appointee and the father of Gregory's own law partner.

One of the strongest attacks on the Supreme Court as "the bulwark of capitalism" came from Gustavus Myers in his 1912 *History of the Supreme Court.* He saw its 1894 decision *In re Debs* as evidence of class bias. This means that he saw it within a view of history as a constant struggle between people that have money and power and those who are powerless. He argued that the prosecution lawyers and the Supreme Court justices wanted the strike and boycott to be crushed so that workers would be kept in their lower economic place. With this as their basic goal, they looked for the best arguments to justify their actions and fool people about their true intentions.

Myers said that "the interests of the Pullman Company and nearly all of the large railroad systems were closely associated;" the success of one company helped the profits of the others. He felt that the courts went after the American Railway Union for "conspiracy in restraint of trade," yet they did nothing to the General Managers' Association for controlling wages.

Myers is among those who found evidence for the conspiracy in the number of prosecuting lawyers and judges who had once worked for railroads. This included the Supreme Court justices. Meyers said the Supreme Court had violated "one of the most fundamental principles of the law" when they would not allow Debs and the American Railway Union to be tried by a jury in a criminal court for the accusations against them of train wrecking and other violence.

Still considered one of the most knowledgeable scholars on the Pullman Strike, Professor Almont Lindsey in 1942 published his book, which was very sympathetic to the labor movement. He saw the Supreme Court's *Debs* decision as a setback to the rights of workers.

Lindsey pointed out that organized labor, however, persisted through the Democratic Party in denouncing government by injunction. He saw progress in the Clayton Anti-Trust Act of 1914 which gave unions some protection from injunctions and expressly exempted them from the application of the 1890 Sherman Anti-Trust Law.

Lindsey ended his history by quoting from the *Railway Times* in August 1894 after the Supreme Court decision on *Debs* in May:

No, it was not a defeat—this ending of the most momentous strike of modern times. It could not be, when we are so near a century that is surely to see the right of the masses take that place in the policies of nations which is now basely devoted to the privileges of classes.

Lindsey was writing before the growing power of labor led to nation-wide strikes such as the coal miners' strike and railroad strike that President Truman had to deal with in 1946. Lindsey had seen the Wagner Act passed, favorable to labor, in 1935. Later would follow The Taft-Hartley (1947) and Landrum-Griffin (1959) Acts that many thought necessary to control the increased power and corruption of labor unions controlled by bosses and organized crime.

Now that you have read this book, what do you think?

Glossary

anarchy: from Greek meaning "without a ruler," this word refers to society in which no one rules, and all do as they think best. *Anarchists* are people who strongly reject any established government and often work to overthrow it by violent means.

arbitration: the settlement of a dispute by a person chosen to hear both sides and to come to a judgment the disputants agree in advance to follow.

bail: money deposited in a court of law to guarantee that an arrested person will show up for trial. The larger the alleged crime, the greater the bail will be. The money is returned after the trial.

blacklist: a list of persons considered troublemakers; an employer who values the list will refuse to hire anyone on it. For example, workers dismissed by their railroad for being involved in a strike were not hired by another railroad. A Pullman employee showed a specific blacklist to the Strike Commission, and they printed it in the report.

boycott: a large organized refusal to do something. For example, the members of the American Railway Union voted to *boycott* Pullman cars on the trains they operated.

They would run the train, but they would not couple the Pullman cars onto the train. The word *boycott* comes from the name of a cruel landlord's agent in 19th century Ireland, Charles Boycott; the people would not look at him or talk to him, making him ineffective and causing him to lose his job.

civil court: trial procedure for the resolution of private disputes such as family problems and contract violations.

criminal court: trial procedure for one accused of violating specific laws that harm others or threaten public safety. The 6th Amendment of the U.S. Constitution guarantees an impartial jury trial for one brought to trial for a criminal offense.

contempt (of court): an act judged to show disrespect for the authority or dignity of a court of law. This includes disobedience of a court order outside of the court room and unruly behavior or dress within the court room.

equity court: trial procedure by lawyers and judges for interpreting and applying law in civil cases upon principles of fairness and according to previous applications called *precedents*. Equity cases differ from civil cases because *relief* (the starting or stopping of some action) is sought rather than a payment of money.

grand jury: a jury, usually more than twelve, that investigates accusations and evidence to determine if the accused should be brought to trial before a petit jury of twelve citizens. *Grand* and *petit* are French words that mean large and small.

indict: to make a legal accusation, bringing a person to trial, usually said of a grand jury. An *indictment* refers to the accusation itself. The pronunciation is not phonetic; say it *in-dight* to rhyme with *in light.*

injunction: an order from a court of law forbidding or ordering an action. Disobedience of an injunction is considered contempt of court.

lay-off: temporary unemployment. A worker expects rehiring when the company can resume full production.

lock-out: a refusal by an employer to let workers into the workplace until problems are resolved.

militia: citizens and former soldiers trained for emergency service in their states. The militia can be ordered by the governor to keep order in the state or by the president to help in a national emergency. The combined state militias are called the National Guard.

monopoly: complete control of a certain kind of goods or service. The word comes from the Greek, meaning "one place only" (to buy things or get a service.) If you play the board game Monopoly, you want to get all the hotels of a certain color so you can build houses and charge higher rents that you couldn't if you didn't own all of that color. When a large railroad bought up smaller ones, people had no competing railroad from whom they could get cheaper rates.

robber barons: originally noblemen in the Middle Ages who robbed travelers passing through their land. In U.S. history the term applies to late nineteenth century capitalists who acquired vast wealth through monopoly, low wages, ruthless financing, and the greedy use of Nature's resources (wood, oil, water, gas, minerals, etc.)

strike: an organized refusal by employees to work unless certain demands are met, usually having to do with wages, hours, or working conditions.

subpoena: an order from a court of law to a person to appear in the court to give testimony. A subpoena is always written and delivered in person. It comes from the Latin phrase "with punishment," and indicates that if a person does not come, he or she may be charged with contempt of court. Pronounce it _suh-pee'-nah._

ukase: in Russia under the Czars, an imperial decree that automatically became law. When Governor Altgeld said that the July 2 injunction was a ukase, he meant that President Cleveland and Attorney General Olney were acting as if they had a czar's power, which they should not have in a democratic republic.

Timeline for the Pullman Strike

(also called the Chicago Strike of 1894)

1864-65 George Pullman patents and builds the Pioneer, the modern railroad sleeping car.

1867 Pullman founds the Pullman Palace Car Company.

1869 Knights of Labor is founded to represent all kinds of laborers.

1877 First major railroad strike is started by Baltimore & Ohio firemen after a ten percent pay reduc tion; it spreads to other Eastern railroads. It col lapses when state and federal troops are called in.

1880-81 Pullman founds the town of Pullman south of Chicago on Lake Calumet as a model commu- nity for workers of his company.

1886 Knights of Labor is reorganized into the American Federation of Labor by Samuel Gompers. General Managers' Association is formed in Chicago by managers from twenty- four rail-roads to establish pay scales for railroad workers.

1893 **May-November** World's Columbian Exposition (also called the Chicago Fair) in honor of 400th anniversary of Columbus' voyage. Financial panic sweeps the country paralyzing industry, causing 3 million workers to lose jobs, and wages to be lowered.

June 20 American Railway Union is founded to unite railway workers in a single organization; Eugene Debs is elected its president. Wages in Pullman Works are greatly reduced, by twenty-five percent average from September 1893 to May 1894.

1894 **March-May** Some Pullman workers join American Railway Union.

April Debs leads successful American Railway Union strike against the Great Northern. A committee of Minneapolis-St. Paul businessmen arbitrates in favor of the workers.

May 7-9 A committee of Pullman workers asks for increased wages/lower rents in Pullman housing.

May 10 Three of the committee are laid off. Forty-six representatives of local union Pullman workers call for a strike vote.

May 11 4000 workers of the Pullman Palace Car strike to protest wage cuts and the perceived firing of union representatives.

June 12-23 The American Railway Union holds convention in Chicago, representing 150,000 members.

June 15-22 Pullman Company refuses 1) communication with ARU and 2) consideration of any arbitration.

June 21 Delegates of American Railway Union vote to stop handling Pullman cars on June 26, if Pullman Company refuses arbitration.

June 22 Pullman Company meets with General Managers' Association and decides to resist the boycott on handling Pullman cars.

June 26 Boycott and accompanying strikes begin and spread as General Managers' Association members discharge men who refuse to handle passenger trains with Pullman cars.

June 28 Complaints of forcible seizures of trains and other violence cause U.S. Attorney General Richard Olney to order U.S. district attorneys to arrest any people engaged in obstruction of trains.

June 30 Chicago district attorney reports disabled mail trains and recommends deputizing of guards to ride the mail trains. Olney suggests application of 1890 Sherman Anti-Trust Act to break the strike in Chicago as a "conspiracy."

July 2 Olney has the Chicago district attorney issue an injunction to Eugene Debs and the American Railway Union: they must not restrain interstate commerce or obstruct the U.S. mail; no one may persuade, encourage, or threaten railway workers to strike. U.S. Army troops at Fort Sheridan prepare to move to Chicago.

July 3 U.S. marshal J.W. Arnold in Chicago reports mobs detaching mail cars, overturning freight cars, controlling railway junctions, etc. and asks for the troops.

July 4 Federal troops arrive in Chicago.

July 5 A mob of 2000 is reported at the Chicago Stock Yards, milling among the troops, obstructing traffic, and derailing a train. Governor Altgeld requests removal of federal troops in a telegram to President Cleveland, stating State troops are in adequate control; he protests Federal supremacy over States' rights.

Buildings in Jackson Park left from the Chicago Fair are set afire.

July 6 700 box cars are burned in the rail yards at Fiftieth Street. A mob stones and shoots at soldiers and crew on a train clearing an obstruction. Illinois militia use bayonets and bullets to break up the mob. Four are killed, twenty wounded.

July 8 President Cleveland issues Executive Proclamation to Chicago for people to cease "unlawful obstructions, combinations, and assemblages and retire peaceably to their respective abodes on or before twelve o'clock noon of the 9th day of July" or face the consequences.

July 10 A federal grand jury finds "conspiracy to obstruct the US mails." Debs and three others are arrested. Militia opens up blockade to the Chicago Stock Yards.

July 12 American Railway Union offers to abandon the strike and boycott if workers are rehired.

July 13 Chicago rail yards are all open and train schedules back to normal. American Railway Union representatives meet with American Federation of Labor officials and conclude the strike is lost. They advise workers to return to work and seek remedy by voting for political candidates sympathetic to labor.

July 17 Debs is arrested a second time for contempt of court in violating the July 2 injunction.

July 18 Strikers return to work at Pullman if they agree not to belong to a union.

July 26 President Cleveland appoints a committee to collect and report the facts about the strike.

August 15 Hearings of U.S. Strike Commission begin in Chicago.

November 14 *Report on the Chicago Strike of June-July, 1894* by the United States Strike Commission presented to President Cleveland. It condemns boycotts, lockouts, and strikes as "barbarism unfit for the intelligence of the age, and as economically considered, very injurious and destructive forces," but states that the "real responsibility for these disorders rests with the people themselves and with the

Government for not adequately controlling monopolies and corporations, and for failing to reasonably protect the rights of labor and redress its wrongs."

December 14 Debs and associates are found guilty of contempt of court.

1895   **January 8** Debs begins six-month jail sentence for contempt.

January 14 Debs appeals to the Supreme Court.

January 24 Debs' conspiracy trial begins in Chicago.

February 12 A juror gets sick and the judge rules he cannot be replaced. The conspiracy trial is never resumed by the prosecution.

May 27 *In re Debs* decision: Supreme Court upholds the right of the U.S. Government to use injunctions and physical force in preventing obstruction of U.S. mails and interstate commerce.

1898   Illinois Supreme Court says that the town of Pullman where all property belongs to a single company is "opposed to good public policy" and orders Pullman Company to sell within five years all property not a part of their factory.

1901   Various socialist wings are united in the Socialist Party of America (with Debs as Presidential candidate in 1904, 1908, 1912, and 1920.)

Bibliography

Altgeld, John P. *Live Questions.* Chicago: published by author, 1899. Excerpt from Speech at Cooper Union, New York, October 17, 1896, reprinted in Warne.

Biographical Directory of the U.S. Congress 1774-1971. Washington: U.S. Government Printing Office, 1971.

Columbia Encyclopedia. Fifth Edition.

Dictionary of American Biography.

Carwardine, William H. *The Pullman Strike.* Chicago: Charles Kerr, 1894. Authorized facsimile. Ann Arbor, Michigan: University Microfilms, 1969.

Cleveland, Grover. *The Government in the Chicago Strike of 1894.* Princeton: Princeton University Press, 1913.

Debs, Eugene V. *Liberty: A Speech Delivered at Battery D Chicago, on Release from Woodstock Jail, November 22, 1895.* Terre Haute: E.V. Debs & Co., 1895.

Edwards, Paul K. *Strikes in the U.S. 1881-1974.* Oxford: Basil Blackwell, 1981.

Howard, Robert P. *Mostly Good and Competent Men: Illinois Governors 1818-1988.* Springfield Illinois: Illinois State Historical Society, 1988.

Husband, Joseph. *The Story of the Pullman Car.* Chicago: A.C. McClurg, 1917.

James, Henry. *Richard Olney and His Public Service.* Boston: Houghton Mifflin, 1923. Excerpt 43-58 reprinted in Warne.

"In re Debs, Petitioner," United States Reports, Vol 158: Cases Adjudged in the Supreme Court at October Term, 1894. New

York: Banks and Brothers, 1895. Excerpts reprinted in Warne 33-38.

King, Willard L. "The Debs Case." Lecture at Amherst College, 19 November 1952. Reprinted in Warne.

Lewis, Oscar. *The Big Four.* New York: Knopf, 1941.

Lindsey, Almont. *The Pullman Strike: The Story of a Unique Experiment and of a Great Labor Upheaval.* Chicago: University of Chicago Press, 1942.

Manning, Thomas G. *The Chicago Strike of 1894: Industrial Labor in the Late Nineteenth Century.* New York: Holt, Rinehart and Winston, 1965.

McCullough, David. *Truman.* New York: Simon and Schuster, 1992.

Myers, Gustavus. *History of the Supreme Court of the United States.* Chicago: Charles H. Kerr, 1912.

Paddock, Lisa. *Facts about the Supreme Court of the United States.* New York: H.H. Wilson, 1996.

Renstrom, Peter G. *The American Law Dictionary.* Santa Barbara CA: ABC-CLIO, 1991.

Stein, Leon, ed. *The Pullman Strike* reprinted in *American Labor: From Conspiracy to Collective Bargaining.* New York: Arno & the New York Times, 1969.

United States Strike Commission. *Report on the Chicago Strike of June-July, 1894.* Washington: Government Printing Office, 1895. Facsimile Reprint. Clifton, N.J.: Augustus M. Kelley Publishers, 1972.

Warne, Colston E. ed. *The Pullman Boycott of 1894: The Problem of Federal Intervention.* Boston: D.C. Heath, 1955.

Index

1893 Depression, 34

Addams, Jane, 83
Altgeld, John Peter, 18-20, 47-48, 50, 61, 91-93
America Federation of Labor (AFL), 15, 89
American Arbitration Association, 91
American Railway Union, 17, 36-38, 40, 43, 53, 55-56, 58, 60-62, 65-66, 69, 71, 75
Arbitration Act, 73
Arnold, J.W., 43, 45
Atchinson, Topeka & Santa Fe, 30, 55
Atchison, F., 36

Baltimore & Ohio, 14, 30
Brennan, Michael, 47

Carnegie Steel Corporation, 14-15
Carnegie, Andrew, 26

Carwardine, William, 36
Central Pacific, 59
Chicago & Alton, 22
Chicago & Northwestern, 30
Chicago & Rock Island, 30
Chicago Record, 82
Chicago, Burlington & Quincy, 30
Civic Federation, 83
Clayton Anti-Trust Act, 96
Cleveland, Grover, 12, 41, 44, 47-48, 50, 53-54, 56, 59, 73, 81, 93-94
Congress of Industrial Organizations, 89
Curtis, Jennie, 82

Darrow, Clarence, 68, 71, 95
Debs, Eugene Victor, 15-18, 21, 35-37, 41, 43, 45, 64-67, 69-72, 88, 92, 94, 96
Dictionary of American Biography, 94

Egan, John, 40, 48
Erie Canal, 21
Equal Rights Amendment, 90

Federal Anti-Injunction Act, 93
Firemen's Magazine, 17

General Managers' Association, 30, 32-33, 38, 40-41, 53, 62, 64, 71, 75-76, 78, 95
Gilbert, Sheriff, 47
Gompers, Samuel, 15
Great Northern, 17-18
Gregory, Stephen Strong, 71, 95
Grosscup, Peter, 65, 67, 69, 94

Haymarket Square Riots, 14, 20
Heathcoate, Thomas, 82
Hill, James J., 17-18
History of the Supreme Court, 95
Homestead Strike, 15
Hopkins, John, 47, 53

Illinois Central, 30, 73, 78

Industrial Workers of the World, 88
Interstate Commerce Act, 43

Kernan, John D., 73, 82-83
King, Willard, 94
Knights of Labor, 14-15

Labor-Management Reporting and Disclosure Act, 93
Lamont, Daniel, 41
Landrum-Griffin Act, 90, 97
Lincoln, Abraham, 24, 94
Lindsey, Almont, 96-97

Milchrist, Thomas, 43, 65
Myers, Gustavus, 95

National Labor Relations Act of 1935, 86
National Labor Relations Board, 91
New York Times, 45
Northern Pacific, 60

Olney, Richard, 41-43, 45, 48, 59-61, 65, 67, 91-95
Our Penal Machinery and Its Victims, 18

Pullman Palace Car
    Company, 9-12, 34-36,
    38, 41, 53, 62, 64-65,
    69, 75-76, 78, 86, 95
Pullman, George, 10-11, 21-
    22, 24, 26, 28, 30, 31,
    35-37, 72, 86-87

Railway Times, 96
Rhodie, Theodore, 82
Rock Island, 60, 73

Schofield, John, 41, 45
Sherman Anti-Trust Law,
    43, 58, 96
Southern Pacific, 58-59

Taft-Hartley Act, 90, 93, 97
Truman, Harry, 97
Trumbull, Lyman, 94

U.S. Strike Commission,
    73-76, 78, 80-84, 86, 88,
    90-91
Union Pacific, 56
United Auto Workers, 89
United Farm Workers, 90

Wagner Act, 86, 91, 97
Western Union, 61, 65

Wood, Mary Alice, 82
Woodruff Sleeping Car
    Company, 22
World's Columbian
    Exposition, 34-35, 50, 80
Worthington, Nicholas E.,
    73, 82
Wright, Carroll D., 73, 82